T0144910

Everest 1951

Everest 1951

The Mount Everest Reconnaissance Expedition

ERIC SHIPTON

Vertebrate Publishing, Sheffield
www.v-publishing.co.uk

Everest 1951

Eric Shipton

 Vertebrate Publishing
Omega Court, 352 Cemetery Road, Sheffield S11 8FT, United Kingdom.
www.v-publishing.co.uk

First published by Hodder & Stoughton, London, 1951. This edition first
published in 2019 by Vertebrate Publishing.

Vertebrate Publishing
Omega Court, 352 Cemetery Road, Sheffield, S11 8UT, UK.

Copyright © Shipton Estate 1951.

Eric Shipton has asserted his rights under the Copyright, Designs and Patents
Act 1988 to be identified as the author of this work.

This book is a work of non-fiction based on the life, experiences and
recollections of Eric Shipton. In some limited cases the names of people,
places, dates and sequences or the detail of events have been changed solely
to protect the privacy of others. The author has stated to the publishers that,
except in such minor respects not affecting the substantial accuracy of the
work, the contents of the book are true.

A CIP catalogue record for this book is available from the British Library.

ISBN 978-1-912560-11-0 (Paperback)
ISBN 978-1-906148-83-6 (Ebook)

All rights reserved. No part of this book covered by the copyright herein may
be reproduced or used in any form or by any means – graphic, electronic, or
mechanised, including photocopying, recording, taping or information storage
and retrieval systems – without the written permission of the publisher.

Every effort has been made to obtain the necessary permissions with
reference to copyright material, both illustrative and quoted. We apologise
for any omissions in this respect and will be pleased to make the appropriate
acknowledgements in any future edition.

Produced by Vertebrate Publishing.

Contents

Foreword
Shipton's Legacy for Mountaineers
By Stephen Venables

Eric Shipton was one of the great mountain explorers of the twentieth century. As a young climber he was brave and skilful, with a prodigious flair for pioneering new routes on remote peaks, far from any hope of rescue. During the course of his life that bold vision broadened to encompass immense landscapes and he was drawn increasingly to the wide canvas of exploration, with the result that we sometimes forget what a brilliant natural climber he was. However, whether we view him as an explorer, or climber, or both, his greatest achievement was to unlock the secrets of so many mountain ranges. The mountains he discovered – and the manner in which he discovered them – remain an inspiration to all who have attempted to follow in his steps.

I first came across his name in 1972. I had just started climbing, I was filled with dreams of far off mountains and was devouring everything I could on the subject. One book in particular seemed to enshrine all my half-formed aspirations. It was Shipton's autobiography, *That Untravelled World*. Here was a man who had dared to follow his dreams and whose sense of enchantment sparkled from every page of unadorned prose.

Soon I got to know all the other books and followed Shipton's travels in more detail, discovering the intricacies of the Nanda Devi adventure, the repeated attempts on Everest and the breathtaking scope of the great Karakoram explorations told in my favourite of all, *Blank on the Map*. I couldn't afford to buy first editions and had to rely on borrowed library copies. So I was delighted when a new omnibus *Eric Shipton: The Six Mountain-Travel Books* assembled all his early narratives into a single affordable volume, complete with well-captioned photos, additional articles, clear maps, pertinent appendices and an eloquent introduction by Jim Perrin. It remains a treasured and constantly rejuvenating source of inspiration.

Since first reading Shipton's books, I have got to know some of the people who actually climbed with him – Scott Russell in the Karakoram, George Lowe and Charles Wylie in Nepal, John Earle in Patagonia. They all found him a delightful companion, a great conversationalist, an enthusiast but also a gently provocative rocker of the establishment. And it's that same engaging personality that speaks through the books; they are immensely readable.

As Jim Perrin points out, the writings would be remarkable if only for their sheer geographical scope. From his astonishingly bold, assured, pioneering debut on Mount Kenya, to Everest, to Garhwal and the Karakoram, to Turkestan, to Patagonia, Shipton's explorations covered immense areas of wilderness. But it was the manner of those explorations that made them such a continuing inspiration to modern mountaineers. Few of us cover as much ground; none of us has equalled the record of the 1935 Everest reconnaissance expedition that made first ascents of twenty-two peaks over 20,000 feet; most of us would baulk at the frugality espoused by Shipton and his famously austere companion, Bill Tilman; but the ideal – of achieving more with less, travelling uncluttered, attuned to the landscape – remains an aspiration.

As Harold Evans famously pointed out, a picture can be worth a thousand words. It was Eric Shipton's 1937 photos of the Latok peaks, the Ogre and Uli Biaho that inspired the next generation. In a sense he threw down the gauntlet for John Roskelley, Doug Scott, Jim Donini and all those others who brought modern techniques to the soaring granite towers in what is now northern Pakistan. More recently the spire that bears Shipton's name has been a recurring magnet for modern American climbers like Greg Child, Mark Synott and Steph Davis. Shipton had the grand vision to reveal vast tracts of previously unexplored mountain country; his modern followers are enjoying the fruits – whether it is the fine detail of a vertical rock tower or the broader sweep of the great Karakoram ski tours carried out by people like Ned Gillete, David Hamilton and the Odier brothers. For myself, with Phil Bartlett and Duncan Tunstall, it was thrilling, in 1987, to try and emulate Shipton, making a serendipitous first ascent above the Biafo Glacier, before continuing over Snow Lake to the same Khurdopin Pass he had reached with Scott Russell forty-eight years earlier, at the outbreak of the Second World War.

That war saw Russell incarcerated in the infamous Changi jail in Singapore, while Shipton languished more comfortably in one of the few proper jobs he ever had – as British Consul in Kashgar. There he wrote his first volume of autobiography, *Upon That Mountain*. He ends the book on an elegiac note, describing his last evening on Snow Lake before returning to a 'civilisation' embarked on a cataclysmic war. 'The great granite spires of the Biafo stood black against a deep blue sky. At least this mountain world, to which I owed so much of life and happiness, would stand above the ruin of human hopes, the heritage of a saner generation of men.'

Elegant prose from a man who, as Peter Steele's excellent 1998 biography revealed, was dyslexic and relied heavily on editorial help from some of his many girlfriends. If only some of today's celebrity adventurer authors could be given similar help. But it's not just down to writing style. All too often the authors are simply ticking lists, notching up goals. With Shipton the journey was everything, the tantalising view into an unknown cirque more important than the prestigious summit. Despite his obvious natural flair as a climber, he became increasingly drawn to the bigger picture, the far horizon. And by all accounts he could be hazy about logistical details. Hence the Everest putsch of 1952, when he lost the leadership of what was likely to be, finally, the successful expedition. The irony was that Shipton had taken part in more Everest expeditions than anyone else alive. As an outraged Charles Wylie pointed out, 'he was *the* man, he was Mr Everest.' Of course, the replacement leader, John Hunt, was in his very different way just as charming and charismatic as Shipton, and he ran a brilliant show. But, as Hunt was the first to acknowledge, it was Shipton who had assembled his crack team, including the two New Zealanders, George Lowe and Ed Hillary, who both played such key roles in 1953. And it was Shipton who had, in 1935, first employed the aspiring young Tibetan, Tenzing Norgay.

Even the most selfless, unworldly saint would be aggrieved at losing his chance of global fame. Shipton had obviously thrilled to the opportunity, in 1951 and 1952, to be first into untouched country along the Nepal-Tibet border, all the way from Makalu to Menlungtse, but for a jobbing mountain lecturer and writer, success on Everest itself would have brought useful kudos. The sense of missed opportunity cannot have been helped by the subsequent break-up of his marriage. For a while he began to resemble a character from a Benjamin Britten opera – an outcast, an oddball, a penniless misfit.

There the story might have ended, had it not been for the redemptive solace of mountain wilderness and the realization of new challenges. Like his former climbing partner Tilman, Shipton began a whole new career of exploration in the far south, rejuvenated by the stark empty spaces of Patagonia and Tierra del Fuego. And here again the world he explored has become a magnet for modern climbers. His gruelling first crossings of the great southern icecaps remain a template for today's sledge-haulers, including his younger son, John Shipton, who is increasingly following in his father's steps. Likewise on Tierra del Fuego, where one of today's most imaginative and ascetic mountaineers, Andy Parkin – and his frequent companion Simon Yates – is drawn repeatedly to the mountain ranges Shipton first unravelled. And on the great spires of Cerro Torre and FitzRoy, virtuosos like Rolando Garibotti, Ermanno Salvaterra, Kelly Cordes and Colin Hayley still exemplify the Shipton ideal of travelling light, paring down, achieving more with less.

As for that most vulgarised of all mountains – Everest; there too, during a golden age of new possibilities in the seventies and eighties, Shipton's ideals were finally realised. The Australian route up the Great Couloir and the Anglo-American-Canadian route up the East Face, which I was lucky enough to join, were both pulled off by a handful of climbers, without oxygen equipment, and without the help of high altitude porters. As for Reinhold Messner's audacious solo ascent of the North Face – or the remarkable forty-one-hour dash up and down the Japanese-Hornbein Couloir by Erhard Loretan and Jean Troillet – they probably exceeded Shipton's wildest imaginings.

There is one other quality – seemingly modern but actually timeless – that many modern climbers share with Eric Shipton, and that is the decision to follow the path of their own choosing. There was a wonderful moment in the early thirties when Shipton realised that expeditioning really could become his life, that he could continue to play this endlessly fascinating game, in his case never losing that vital sense of curiosity. That is what makes these books so compelling to every generation that follows. As he wrote in his coda to *Upon That Mountain*:

> There are few treasures of more lasting worth than the experiences of a way of life that is in itself wholly satisfying. Such, after all, are the only possessions of which no fate, no cosmic catastrophe can deprive us; nothing can alter the fact if for one moment in eternity we have really lived.

Stephen Venables, June 2010

1 The Project

When, in 1924, Norton and Somervell so nearly reached the summit of Mount Everest, it was generally believed that the next expedition, taking advantage of the lessons they had learned, would most probably succeed. For, just as the 1922 parties, by attempting to climb the last 4,000 feet to the top in a single day, had completely underestimated the physiological difficulties of climbing at great altitudes, so it seemed that the failure of the 1924 expedition was due to a simple, avoidable cause. That year the climbers had gone high too soon and had become involved in a series of struggles with the early spring blizzards, which had so far drained their strength that, when the time came to launch their attempts upon the summit, the climbers were already exhausted. In 1933 we were confident that, by carefully nursing the climbers and the Sherpas chosen to go high through the preliminary stages and by the use of comfortable, double-skinned tents at Camps 3 and 4, it would be possible to place several successive parties at a camp above 27,000 feet, with their reserves of strength largely unimpaired, and well able to overcome the last 2,000 feet.

Once again we found that we had under-rated the resources of our opponent. We had been led by the experiences of the previous expedition to assume that at the end of May and beginning of June there would be a period of some two weeks of calm weather before the monsoon wrapped the mountain in a blanket of snow. Moreover, we had not fully realised the extent to which even a small deposit of new snow upon the rocks of the final pyramid would render them unclimbable. Our experiences in the 1930s showed all too clearly that such a spell of favourable conditions immediately before the monsoon could not be relied upon. Indeed, it did not occur in any of the three years when attempts were made during that decade. In 1933 we had perhaps a fleeting chance, but both in 1936 and 1938 the monsoon was upon us before we had even established a camp on the North Col.

Even now we cannot assess the chances in any given year of meeting with a sufficiently late – or, as we used to think 'normal' – monsoon to ensure favourable conditions for reaching the top. We cannot say, from the evidence we have, whether 1924 was an exceptional year, recurring perhaps only once or twice in a generation, or whether in the 1930s we perhaps encountered a limited cycle of unfavourable seasons. Whatever the answer, it seemed that the problem of reaching the summit of Mount Everest from the north had been reduced to this one vital question. Three times men had climbed to more than 28,000 feet, unaided by oxygen apparatus; we believed that the climbing on the last thousand feet was no more difficult than that which had already been accomplished, but it was sufficiently difficult to demand good conditions of weather and snow; given these, there seemed to be no reason for failure, without them success would not be attained. Had it been possible, the obvious solution would have been to send out a small party each successive year until the right conditions occurred. There would have been no lack of personnel, and the modest expense would have been amply justified by physiological and other scientific research. Unfortunately, permission to do this could not be obtained from the Tibetan Government.

The attempt to climb Mount Everest, once an inspiring adventure, had become little more than a gambler's throw. To overcome this unhappy situation we had begun, as long ago as 1935, to consider the possibility of finding an alternative approach which would present a different kind of problem, one not so completely dependent for success upon the date of the monsoon.

From the mountains above the Kangshung Glacier, to the south-east, we had seen the ridge running up to the summit from the gap (the 'South Col') between Everest and Lhotse. This clearly offered a much easier route up the final pyramid than that across the treacherous slabs of the North Face. It was broad and not so steep, while the dip of the strata would favour the climber. But was there any way of reaching the South Col? We had seen that the eastern side was impossible. The western side of the Col was unknown ground.

The Reconnaissance Expedition of 1921 had discovered in broad outline the geography of the south-western side of Mount Everest. The three great peaks of the massif, Everest, Lhotse (South Peak) and Nuptse (West Peak), together with their high connecting ridges, enclosed a basin which Mallory named the West Cwm. (Mallory had climbed a great deal in North Wales and for that reason he used the Welsh spelling of the word 'combe'.) Any approach to the South Col must lie up this hidden valley, which enclosed the whole of the southern aspect of Mount Everest.

On the 1935 Reconnaissance Expedition, when, with no intention of attempting to climb Everest, we had before us a wide field of mountain travel, our programme included an attempt to find a way to the West Cwm from the north. From the Lho La at the head of the Rongbuk Glacier, and also from a high col on the main watershed farther to the west, where we camped for two nights, we had close views of the entrance to the Cwm, a narrow defile flanked on the south by the great face of Nuptse and on the north by the western shoulder of Everest. Between these lofty portals the glacier of the Cwm poured in a huge icefall, a wild cascade of ice blocks, 2,000-feet high. The upper part of the Cwm was screened from view by a northerly bend in the valley, so that we could not see either the South Col or the south face of

Everest; nor could we find a practicable route down the precipices on the southern side of the watershed which would have enabled us to reach the foot of the icefall.

Thus the possibility of finding an alternative route up Mount Everest from the south-west could not be put to the test, for the only way of approaching the mountain from that side was through the valley of Sola Khumbu in Nepal.

That country had long been forbidden to Western travellers and there was, in those days, no chance of obtaining permission from the Government of Nepal to send an expedition to that area. Since the war, however, the Nepalese Government began to relax their policy of rigid exclusion, and from 1947 onwards several mountaineering and scientific expeditions – American, French and British – were permitted to visit various parts of the Nepal Himalaya. In the autumn of 1950, Dr Charles Houston and his father, together with H.W. Tilman, paid a brief visit to the upper valleys of the Khumbu district. Houston and Tilman spent a day exploring the glacier flowing southward from the Lho La, but did not have time to reach the icefall.

In May 1951, Michael Ward proposed to the Himalayan Committee (a joint committee of the Royal Geographical Society and the Alpine Club, which has handled all previous Everest Expeditions) that permission should be sought for a British expedition to go to Everest that autumn. His suggestion was energetically supported by Campbell Secord and W.H. Murray; formal permission was applied for and, on the assumption that it would be forthcoming, Murray began the preliminary work of organising the expedition. I was in China at the time, and when I arrived home in the middle of June I had no idea of what was afoot; indeed, nothing was farther from my thoughts than taking part in a Himalayan expedition. After I had been in England for about ten days, I went to London and happened to call on Secord. He said, 'Oh, you're back, are you? What are you going to do now?' I told him that I had no plans, to which he replied, 'Well, you'd better lead this expedition.' I said, 'What expedition?' and he explained the position.

At first, I did not take the suggestion very seriously, for it seemed that, owing to the recent political disturbances in Nepal, it was unlikely that permission for an expedition would be forthcoming. But within a few days the Committee heard that, through the courtesy of the Nepali Government and the good offices of Mr Christopher Summerhayes, the British Ambassador at Kathmandu, permission for the expedition had been granted. I found the decision to join the expedition a very difficult one to make. Having so lately emerged from Communist China, the freedom of England and the absence of suspicion, hatred and fear, were sheer delight, and the English summer a rare and treasured experience. I found it hard to leave all this and my family again almost immediately. Moreover, I had been away so long from the world of mountaineering that I doubted my value to the expedition.

3

On the other hand, for twenty years, ever since I had first known the Sherpas, I had longed, above all else, to visit their land of Sola Khumbu, through which the expedition would travel. I had heard so much about it from the Sherpas; indeed during our journeys together in other parts of the Himalaya and Central Asia, whenever we came upon a particularly attractive spot, they invariably said, 'This is just like Sola Khumbu,' and the comparison always led to a long, nostalgic discourse about their homeland. It required only an intelligent glance at the map and a little imagination to realise that their praise was not exaggerated; moreover, we had looked down into the upper valleys of Khumbu from the peaks west of Everest. Almost unknown to Western travellers, it had become, to me at least, a kind of Mecca, an ultimate goal in Himalayan exploration. So it was that I finally decided to accept the invitation to lead the expedition.

The possibility of finding a new approach to the summit of Mount Everest from the south-west had assumed a new significance to mountaineers all over the world from the time when the impending 'liberation' of Tibet by the Chinese Communist armies had made the old line of approach inaccessible to citizens of Western countries. It was, however, highly improbable that such an alternative existed. No experienced mountaineer can be optimistic about the chances of finding a way up any great Himalayan peak. The vast scale of which these giants are built greatly increases the likelihood of the climber being faced by sheer impossibility – an unclimbable wall, slopes dominated by hanging glaciers, or avalanche-swept couloirs. In addition, his standard of performance is greatly reduced; the fact that heavy loads have to be carried a long way up the mountain to establish camps, the physical disabilities resulting from altitude, the disastrous consequences which threaten from bad weather – these are some of the factors which usually make it impossible for him to accept the challenge of a difficult ridge or face, or to commit himself to a spell of many hours of really hard climbing. When, as in this case, the search for a route is confined to one particular segment of the mountain, the chances of finding a practicable route are obviously still further reduced.

All that we knew of the South Face of Mount Everest and of the western side of the South Col was that they must be approached up a formidable icefall and through a narrow defile which was probably menaced by ice avalanches from the hanging glaciers on the immense precipices above. Beyond the defile was the unknown Cwm, whose southern containing wall, the 25,000-foot ridge connecting Lhotse with Nuptse, obscured all but the very summit of Everest from the south. We estimated that the floor of the Cwm was about 21,000 feet high, nearly 5,000 feet below the crest of the South Col. From the fact that, along the whole range, the mountains were far steeper on the southern side of the watershed than on the northern side, we inferred that the slopes below the col would not be easy. That was all we could guess. It did not present a picture upon which we could build great hopes. But the West Cwm was a freak of mountain architecture and there was no knowing what we might find there. I put the chances against our finding a practicable route at about thirty to one.

Clearly the expedition could only be a reconnaissance; moreover, the time and money at our disposal were not sufficient to organise an attempt to climb the mountain. If, despite the long odds, we found a possible route, we naturally hoped to send a further expedition the following spring to attempt it; for we still believed that, despite its many disadvantages, the spring was the only time of year to tackle the mountain. A case had been argued for making the attempt in the late autumn; that is, after the monsoon instead of before it. So far as I know, this idea had not gained the support of anyone who had been high on the mountain, but it had never been put to a practical test. There were many conflicting theories about the weather and snow conditions likely to be encountered in the autumn; there was little evidence on which to base these theories, and what evidence there was seemed equally conflicting. By visiting the mountain after the monsoon we hoped to furnish answers to some of these questions.

Preparations for the expedition had to be made in a great hurry. It was already July before I had made up my mind to go, and stores and equipment had to be ready for shipment to India by the end of that month. Before the war I used to boast that I could organise a Himalayan expedition in a fortnight. Things had changed since then. Essential materials for equipment, such as eiderdown for sleeping bags, windproof cloth and rope, were in short supply, and manufacturing firms were busy with priority orders. Whereas before the war it was possible at a moment's notice to obtain passages and cargo space on any of several ships sailing for India each week, especially in the off-season when we usually travelled, now sailings were infrequent and the ships always full. It seemed as though everyone we tried to contact was away on holiday. The problem of raising money to finance the expedition had to be solved quickly. It was a busy and confusing month, and there was little time to enjoy the summer woods at home. Fortunately, Bill Murray had done a great deal of the ground work already, and Campbell Secord allowed his house in Carlton Mews to be used as a dumping ground for stores and equipment as they accumulated. This was very hard on his wife, for the place became a sort of general office and Mrs Secord had to bear the brunt of endless telephone calls from the press, equipment firms, applicants for a place in the party, inventors of helicopters and portable radio sets, food cranks, money lenders and members of the expedition. I remember especially the day before our stuff was due to go to the docks; nothing had been packed and we were still hopelessly involved in outside business such as arranging for equipment ordered from abroad to pass from the airport to the docks. I sent an SOS to the WVS to ask if they could send someone to come and pack for us. They responded promptly and worked with such efficiency that everything was packed and listed before evening.

The party had originally consisted of Bill Murray, Michael Ward, Tom Bourdillon and Alfred Tissieres, one of the best-known Swiss climbers, who happened to be doing research work in Cambridge at the time. It was also hoped that Campbell Secord would be able to join the party. In its conception it was a purely private party, and, as I have said, the initiative lay with Ward, Murray and Secord. Unfortunately, in the end, neither Tissieres nor Secord were able to accompany the expedition. When I was invited to take over the leadership, I stipulated that the Himalayan Committee should assume complete responsibility for financing the expedition and for all matters connected with press coverage. My reason for this was that, although private expeditions have a very great deal to recommend them, Everest expeditions attract a quite disproportionate amount of public interest, so that publicity requires a firm controlling hand. The Himalayan Committee entered into a contract with *The Times* for the publication and the syndication abroad of the official articles and dispatches dealing with the expedition. By this generous contract, *The Times* provided the bulk of the expedition's funds.

Murray and Ward sailed from Tilbury on 2 August 1951, taking with them all the stores and equipment. They reached Bombay on the 18th. Bourdillon and I flew to Delhi, arriving there on 19 August. Two days before I left London a cable was received from the president of the New Zealand Alpine Club asking whether two members of the New Zealand Expedition, which was climbing in the Garhwal Himalaya that summer, might accompany our party. I also received a request from the Geological Survey of India to attach one of their officers, Dr Dutt, to the expedition. I welcomed these suggestions.

2 The March

From India there are four ways of reaching Namche Bazar, the principal village in the district of Khumbu, where we proposed to make our base. The route from Darjeeling, generally used by the Sherpas, is long and very difficult during the monsoon. The route from Kathmandu, though easier, is also rather long, while the cost in time and money of transporting a large quantity of baggage from India to the Nepali capital would be considerable. By far the quickest way would be from Jainagar, the railhead north of Darbhanga in Bihar. But we were advised that it would be impossible to get from there to the foothills by lorry during the rains, while to march through the hot, swampy country would be most unpleasant. So we decided to travel from Jogbani, another railhead in North Bihar further to the east. Houston's party had gone by this route the previous year after the monsoon was over, and they had succeeded in reaching Namche in a fortnight from Jogbani.

Bourdillon and I reached Jogbani shortly before midnight on 24 August. We were met at the station by a jeep belonging to the Biratnagar Jute Mills. It was raining hard and, judging by the sodden state of the ground all round the little station, it seemed that it had been doing so for weeks. The road was so deep in mud that it took an hour to go from the station to the house of Mr Law, the Chief Engineer of the Jute Mills, less than a mile away. This journey took us across the frontier into Nepali territory. Mr and Mrs Law with Murray and Ward, who had arrived two days before, were waiting up for us. We were given a wonderful welcome in this Scottish home. The following day Colonel Proud, First Secretary of the British Embassy at Kathmandu, arrived. He had been sent by the Ambassador to assist us and to accompany us as far as Dhankuta. His help was invaluable. He had brought with him Lieutenant Chandra Bahadur, an officer of the Nepali Army, whose services had kindly been lent to the expedition.

On the 25th, too, Angtharkay arrived from Darjeeling. He is a very old friend of mine. We had been together on eight Himalayan expeditions before the war, and I had always regarded him as a man of quite outstanding character and ability. During the past few years he had set up a business in Darjeeling organising treks in Sikkim for visitors. But he still went with major expeditions, though now as a Sirdar, or foreman. He was on the French expedition to Annapurna, and climbed to their highest camp. I had asked him to meet us in

Jogbani so as to help with the transport to Namche, and later, of course, for work on the mountain. I had not seen him since 1939, when he was just a simple Sherpa porter, though a famous one, drawing the same pay as the others and carrying the same load. Now he had graduated to a different sphere. I was somewhat apprehensive of what I would find; for success tends to spoil these simple people at least as readily as it does the sophisticated. He had cut off the handsome pigtail that he used to wear and his clothes were distressingly smart, but I was relieved to find the same shy reticence and the same quiet humour that I remembered so well. There was no sign of dissipation and he looked no older; indeed, he had changed remarkably little in the last twelve years. It was curious that, in spite of his constant contact with Europeans, he had learnt practically no English.

Angtharkay had brought with him from Darjeeling twelve Sherpas, including a woman. They were all on their way to Sola Khumbu and were hoping to 'work their passage' with us. We signed on four of them for the duration of the expedition and agreed to employ the others for the march at the same rates of pay as we gave to the local porters.

The next stage of our journey was a lorry drive of thirty miles to Dharan at the foot of the hills. We were told that with all the rain then falling the road would be impassable and that we would have to wait until the weather cleared. This was depressing news, for there seemed to be no reason why it should ever stop raining, though Mr Law assured us that it would. In the meantime we were busy sorting out stores and equipment and packing them into sixty-pound loads for the march. Mr and Mrs Law were very kind and helped in a great many ways, from arranging supplies of kerosene to sewing on buttons and mending socks. Another very pleasant contact we made was with Mr B.P. Koirala, Home Minister of the Government of Nepal, and Mr J.M. Shrinagesh, the Indian Political Adviser, who were setting out on a tour of Eastern Nepal.

On the evening of the 26 August it stopped raining and on the following morning a watery sun shone through the clouds. We set out in our hired lorry at two-thirty that afternoon. At Biratnagar, two miles away, there was an hour's delay while the driver collected supplies of petrol and tinkered with the engine. The lorry was besieged by people wanting a lift to Dharan, and by the time we left it was grossly overloaded. The road was in a deplorable state. Every few hundred yards the vehicle was brought to a standstill in deep mud, and each time we had first to dig trenches to free the wheels and then to spread bundles of grass and jute husks over the mud. It took us more than two hours to cover the first six miles. However, though it started to rain heavily again, conditions improved as we approached the hills. We reached Dharan long after dark, found a billet in an empty house and, after a long search, procured a meal in the bazaar.

The next morning we recruited coolies for the first part of the march. We found that the local practice was to pay coolies so much per seer (two pounds) per stage. The men, therefore, preferred to carry eighty-pound loads instead of sixty pounds, and we had to set about rearranging all our carefully packed baggage. While we were doing this a small boy came and asked if he could be signed on as 'half a coolie.' This tickled the Sherpas, and we gave him a box weighing forty pounds. He carried it so well that later I came to regret that all our porters were not boys.

These matters occupied the whole of the morning, and it was two o'clock in the afternoon before we began the first march. In a couple of miles we reached the foot of the hills. Here, as elsewhere throughout the length of the Himalayas, they rose abruptly from the plains for about 5,000 feet to the crest of the first range of foothills. We walked with our umbrellas up, for the sun was shining at last and it was very hot; but after a couple of hours we had climbed into low-hanging clouds where the air was deliciously cool and fresh. We spent the night in a small village just below the crest of the first range and started on at dawn on the 29 August. It had rained heavily all night, but now it had cleared somewhat, and as we crossed the ridge we had a glimpse of the Everest and Makalu massifs, seventy-five miles to the north, shining through a rift in the rain clouds. From the pass we descended 3,500 feet to the Tamur River and then climbed a similar height up the other side of the valley to Dhankuta, where we were provided with a tiny rest-house in a pleasant wood of tall pine trees. The following morning Colonel Proud started back on his journey to Jogbani.

Though we had covered a considerable distance, those first two marches had been very easy. The path was wide and well constructed, the porters had gone well and it had not rained at all during the day. So far, we had experienced nothing of the exasperation, the dismal toil of travel through the Himalayan foothills at the height of the monsoon. We soon began to suspect that it was not all going to be so easy. We had hoped that we would be able to persuade the Dharan coolies to remain with us, so that we could continue the march the very next day; but they refused and insisted on being paid off. What was worse, we had the very greatest difficulty in finding any fresh recruits. We sent the Sherpas into the bazaar and the Bara Hakim (local governor) sent peons into the outlying villages to engage the men. A few men arrived and agreed to go with us; but, finding that we were not ready to start, they drifted off again and disappeared. When this had happened several times, the situation began to seem desperate. By the time we had been in Dhankuta for forty-eight hours we felt as though we would never be on our way again. Various plausible but unhelpful explanations were advanced by the local authorities for the lack of coolies: a large military camp had been established nearby, and all the coolies were required to work there; owing to the recent disturbances in the country,

the peasants were frightened to go far from their villages; because of the late-
ness of the rains, work on the land had fallen into arrears, with the result that
the demand for labour was unusually heavy; no one ever travelled far during
the monsoon if he could help it. Looking back, I would say that the last was the
most likely explanation.

We could get curiously little information about the route ahead, and none
that was reliable. We decided that a place called Dingla was to be our next
objective. The country beyond that was, locally, a mere legend. Each person
we asked held a different opinion as to how we should get to Dingla, while
estimates of the time it would take varied between one day and a week.

It is remarkable at such times how, when the situation seems hopeless, all at
once a solution presents itself. At about noon on the 1st September we suddenly found that there were no fewer than seventeen coolies who were willing,
though somewhat half-heartedly, to talk business. We required twenty-five;
but Angtharkay urged that we should start at once with the seventeen before
they had time to change their minds, and that he should follow with the
remaining eight when he could get them. I was reluctant to split the party at
such an early age, but it was obviously the wisest course to follow. Furthermore,
the news that the expedition had moved on would certainly have a quick
psychological effect upon the local carriers, who would immediately begin to
think that they were missing a good thing.

Before starting, we went to say goodbye to the Bara Hakim and to thank him
for his help and hospitality. He had just received a message from Jogbani to say
that the two New Zealanders, E.P. Hillary and H.E. Riddiford, had arrived
there. This was good news, for until then we had had no word of their wherea-
bouts. We sent messages back to them and started on our way. In the evening
we reached a ridge, some 6,000-feet high, overlooking the vast basin of the
Arun River, where we spent the night in the little village of Paribas. Angtharkay
arrived early the following morning. As we had expected, he had found no
difficulty, once we had gone, in recruiting the remaining eight porters. Our
march that day took us 5,000 feet down to the banks of the Arun.

At dawn on 3 September we walked along a wide shore to a place called
Legua Ghat, where there is a primitive ferry. A light mist hung low over the
great river: this began to disperse as soon as the sun was up and we saw, far
away up the valley, the gleam of snow peaks. The ferry consisted of a tree trunk
hollowed out to make a clumsy canoe. It had a crew of three, two paddlers
forward and a steersman aft, and could take seven passengers at one time, or
an equivalent weight of baggage. As soon as the boat was cast off from the
bank it was swept down by the current at an alarming speed. The paddlers
worked furiously to get their frail craft across the river with a minimum loss of
distance, for after each crossing it had to be towed laboriously back along the
shore. The river was about 300 yards wide, and though there were no rapids

for a mile or so downstream which allowed a substantial margin of error, the operation required considerable skill. It took from 7 a.m. until 2 p.m. to complete the ten double crossings necessary to transport ourselves, our coolies and our baggage across the river.

We were now less than 1,000 feet above sea level, and when we resumed the march that afternoon the heat was intense. There was no clearly defined route across the vast forested slopes of the valley. We made our way through steep rocky nullahs along a series of tiny tracks, which, branching and intersecting, connect the scattered hamlets. Often the tracks were so obscure that we lost them. The porters, carrying eighty-pound loads, went very slowly; even so, their speeds varied a great deal and it was impossible to keep everyone together. Thus, with such a diversity of tracks we soon lost contact with some sections of the party. At nightfall on 3 September we reached a hamlet called Komaltar. Though it was only four and a half miles in a direct line from the ferry, it had taken nearly five hours to cover the distance. Nine of the local porters bivouacked in a streambed half a mile short of the hamlet and came in early next morning. The rest failed to turn up and, after sending back in search of them without success, we concluded that they had taken a different route. They reached Dingla more than a day after us.

For seven or eight miles we kept fairly close to the banks of the Arun, sometimes following a stretch of shore. The tropical forest and the dense undergrowth, the birds, the brilliantly coloured locusts, butterflies and other insects were typical of the deep river valleys of the Eastern Himalaya. We wore only shorts and sandshoes, with umbrellas to protect our heads from the heat. Whenever we came to a safe backwater, we used to plunge straight in and sit down for a few moments. The water was deliciously cool, though the refreshing effect did not last long. Even the Sherpas, who are afraid of water and who normally never immerse their bodies, began, at first timidly, then with great zest, to follow suit; all except poor Lhakpa, the woman, who looked on with obvious envy.

On the afternoon of 4 September we climbed 3,000 feet up through lovely country to a cluster of villages called Phalikot, and on the 5th, a relatively short march took us to Dingla, a large, scattered village perched among woods and terraced fields on a high ridge which commanded sweeping views across the Arun basin and, when the weather was clear, of the great snow ranges to the north.

At Dingla we again had great difficulty in recruiting porters. The Dhankuta men had been engaged as far as Dingla and refused to go any farther. We were delayed for four days. On 8 September, Hillary and Riddiford arrived. We now required forty local coolies, for, besides the baggage brought by the New Zealanders, we had bought a quantity of rice and flour in case of a possible shortage in the country beyond. At last, on the evening of the 9th, after long and exasperating negotiations, enough men had been engaged. We gave them an advance of pay, and they promised to be ready to start soon after dawn the next day. But the next morning it was raining very heavily and they did not come until noon. However, after a couple of hours of tumult and confusion, we managed to allot them their loads and get them off.

Our next objective was the Salpa Bhanjyang, a 12,000-foot pass to the north-west leading over from the Arun basin to that of the Hongu Khola. The direct route was impassable owing to some steep mountain streams which were in spate and had swept away the bridges crossing them. This meant that we had to make a long detour to the south-west so as to reach the crest of the high watershed ridge, which we then followed to the pass. The detour cost us several extra days' marching. It was particularly annoying to discover that, if we had known this before, we could have reached the ridge much more quickly by travelling direct to it from Dhankuta via Bojhpur.

On 10 September we made our way along the path leading towards Bojhpur. This was easy and fairly level, but we had started so late and the porters went so slowly that by nightfall we had only reached the village of Phaldobala, four miles away. The next morning the porters refused to go on, saying that their loads were too heavy. According to the local custom, we had contracted to pay them by weight, and for this reason they had in the first place chosen to carry eighty pounds each rather than sixty pounds. This meant that we had once again to rearrange all the loads and also to recruit more porters to carry the surplus. These operations, made no easier by the rain, occupied the whole of that day.

On the march to Dingla it had rained mostly at night and the days had been fine. This happy arrangement could not be expected to last, and by now it was raining for most of each day. We set off again on the morning of the 12th and climbed to the crest of the high, narrow watershed ridge. For three days we made our way slowly along it in a northerly direction, unable to see anything of our surroundings because of alternating spells of heavy rain and equally drenching Scotch mist. After a while we lost all sense of direction and distance; it was a curious sensation, blindly following this narrow crest, the ground on either hand falling steeply into the silent, forested depths below, while rocky peaks loomed, one after another, ahead. The undergrowth was infested with leeches; on a single twig a score of the creatures could be seen, stiff and erect, like a cluster of little black sticks, ready to attach themselves to our legs and arms and clothing as we brushed past.

The way consisted of a continuous series of long, steep climbs and descents. It was very hard work for the porters, for the track was slimy with mud and they slipped constantly, losing their balance under the shifting weight of their sodden loads. We spent the nights in little cowherds' shelters, mostly deserted, which were interspersed along the ridge. They kept out most of the rain, and fires lit inside discouraged the leeches from entering. Without them our lot would have been a great deal worse. One evening at sunset the mists slid down below the ridge, and for a while we saw, across a wide gulf of cloud, the great range of ice peaks.

At the Salpa Bhanjyang, which we reached on the morning of the 15th, we joined the route used by the Sherpas travelling between Khumbu and Darjeeling. Angtharkay told me that when he was last there, in December, 1947, it was so deep in snow that he had taken three days to cross it and that several Sherpas had died attempting to do so. It was a great help at last to have someone in the party who knew the way. From the pass we descended steeply for 7,000 feet to the Hongu Khola. At the village of Bung, on the farther side of the valley, we heard that the bridge across the next big river, the Inukhu Khola, had been washed away, and we had to choose between making a detour of three days to the south or attempting to build another bridge ourselves. We decided on the latter alternative.

From Bung we crossed another pass, about 10,600-feet high, to Khiraunle, which stands about 1,000 feet above the Inukhu Khola. Here we were told that several villages in the neighbourhood had been smitten by an epidemic of some virulent disease which killed its victims in four days. From a description of the symptoms, it seemed probable that it was bubonic plague. There was a village straight across the valley where fifty people had died during the past fortnight. The intervening gorge was so narrow that, though the place was the best part of a day's march away, we could with the naked eye see people moving about in it. We studied their movements with field glasses and saw that they were engaged in some activity which the Sherpas declared was a burial ceremony.

But the village of Khiraunle also provided some less depressing news. The local people were engaged in building a temporary bridge across the Inukhu Khola to take the place of the one that had been washed away, and this would be ready early the following morning. That day was the worst of the march. Heavy rain fell almost continuously. A way had to be cut through the dense undergrowth to enable the porters to climb down the precipitous slopes of the gorge to the point where the new bridge was built. This was only a few hundred yards downstream from the old bridge, but the intervening distance was impassable along the riverbed. The new structure was a very flimsy affair, built in two sections, each spanning a formidable cataract and connecting one bank of the river with a central island. Each section was composed of two slender tree trunks, lashed together with green bark, and a bamboo handrail that would not have withstood a pressure of ten pounds. The river was rising rapidly, and before everyone was across, waves were splashing over the logs. Not long afterwards both sections of the bridge had been swept away, leaving the bamboo handrails flapping crazily in the spray.

We then had to climb a steep cliff to regain the track. In doing this we disturbed a hornets' nest. Not having been attacked myself, I was mystified by the ensuing confusion and panic until the party had reassembled on the track, 300 feet above the river. Two of the coolies had been stung so severely (one claimed seven stings) that they were already suffering from acute fever. Several others had swollen faces and eyes, while one man had disappeared. His load was located near the hornets' nest, and we thought that he had fallen down the cliff in his attempt to escape. I sent Angtharkay on to a village 2,000 feet above to get help, while Bourdillon, Ward and I climbed down the cliffs again and searched along the shore for the missing man, expecting to find his broken corpse. He had not fallen, however, and eventually he was found in a high fever sheltering in a cave. All the victims of this curious encounter recovered overnight.

The next day, the 19th, we crossed another 10,000-foot pass which took us into the valley of the Dudh Kosi. On the evening of 20 September the weather suddenly cleared and the monsoon seemed to have ended. After ten days of perpetual rain and mist, the clear air and warm sunlight were delicious. The forest was no longer oppressive, but light and green; the waterfalls sparkled as they cascaded down the precipices flanking the wide valley, threads of silver hanging from the ice spires 12,000 feet above our heads.

We were now in the country of the Sherpas, and a form of 'Channel fever' animated Angtharkay and his companions. At each village through which we passed they were greeted by a crowd of their friends who took them off to some house to be fed and wined, to the accompaniment of eager chatter and full-blooded laughter. Of course, we came in for our share of this hospitality, which doubtless contributed to the magic of the scene. I began to wonder if, when eventually we reached our objective, any of us would be in a fit state to climb.

The valley split into two narrow gorges. The path, by a remarkable series of log platforms and ladders built in the cliff, followed the right-hand branch for half a mile, the lovely snow peak of Taweche framed between the vertical sides of the canyon, then climbed, zigzag, for 2,000 feet to the intervening ridge. Here, in a little fold in the mountainside, was Namche Bazar, 12,200 feet above sea level. We arrived there in the afternoon of 22nd September. The journey from Jogbani, which we had expected to cover in a fortnight, had taken us nearly four weeks.

Namche Bazar, which consists of about sixty houses, is the most important village in the district of Khumbu, for it is the last place of any size on the principal route from Eastern Nepal to Tibet, and is therefore a centre of trade between the two countries. It is the small metropolis of the Sherpas, who have close connections, both commercial and religious, with Tibet. They are themselves of Tibetan origin and are indistinguishable from the people of the great plateau to the north of the main range. They wear the same kind of clothes and have the same religious beliefs and customs, and, though they have a language of their own, they can all speak Tibetan. They lead a semi-nomadic life; each family owns a house and land in several villages at different altitudes and they move en masse from one village to another according to the seasons, to sow or harvest their fields of potatoes and barley. For this reason, it is common to find a village temporarily deserted while the inhabitants are working at another at a different level. They graze their sheep and goats and yaks in the high valleys, often several days' march from their villages.

We were given a great welcome in Namche, where we spent two days sorting out our stores and equipment and arranging for supplies of local food. I met many old friends from former expeditions, most of whom brought flagons of chang and stood by urging us to drink. We were provided with a house. Nearly all Sherpa houses are built on the same pattern. They are oblong, two-storied stone buildings, with carved wooden window frames and lattice windows. The front door leads into a dark stable, through which one has to grope, pushing past the oxen or yaks, to a steep wooden ladder leading to a short, narrow passageway on the upper floor. A right-hand turn at the top of the ladder leads to a latrine, a small dark room, with a hole in the middle of the floor which is otherwise deeply covered with grass or pine needles. The other end of the passage leads to the living room, which occupies three-quarters of the upper floor. The alcove between the walled-in ladderway and the front wall is used as a kitchen. The fireplace is set on the floor, and an iron frame is used for holding the cooking pots above the fire. Beyond this is a couch reserved for the women. In the front wall to the right of the fireplace there is a line of windows. Beneath this a platform raised about a foot above the floor is covered with carpets and rugs. Here the men sit, cross-legged, behind a low wooden table. The seat of honour is at the end of the platform nearest the fire. The opposite wall, devoid of windows, is lined with shelves, full of great copper basins, wooden bowls, china cups, bamboo churns, and other cooking and eating utensils. The far end of the room is cluttered with bags of grain, ropes, wooden ploughs, mattocks and other farm implements. Beds are made up on the floor as they are required. Some houses belonging to well-to-do people have additional rooms furnished as small Buddhist shrines.

3 The Icefall

We left Namche on 25 September, taking with us supplies for seventeen days. In that time we hoped to make a thorough reconnaissance of the great icefall; if possible, to climb it into the West Cwm and to see whether or not there was a practicable route from there to the South Col. If we found a route we would then send down for more supplies, carry a camp into the cwm and climb as far as possible towards the col. If, as we expected, there proved to be no practicable route, we would then undertake an extensive exploration of the main range, the southern side of which was almost entirely unknown. We had engaged another five Sherpas, whom we equipped for work on the mountain, bringing the number up to ten. One of them was Angtharkay's young brother, Angphuter, whom I had last met in 1938, when as a lad of fourteen he had come across to Rongbuk from Namche and had carried a load to Camp 3 (21,000 feet) on Everest. Another fifteen men had been engaged to carry our baggage and supplies to our Base Camp at the head of the Khumbu Glacier.

We followed a path across the steep mountainside, 2,000 feet above the gorge of the Dudh Kosi, from which we had climbed three days before. On the way we met a very old friend of mine, Sen Tensing, whom I first met in 1935, when he had come across to Tibet to join the reconnaissance expedition. His peculiar appearance in the clothes we gave him had earned him the name of the 'Foreign Sportsman'. In the years that followed he had been my constant companion in various parts of the Himalaya and Karakoram. In 1936 I had taken him to Bombay, an adventure which he evidently still regarded as one of the highlights of his career. He had heard news of our approach while herding his yaks in a valley, three days' march away, and had hurried down to meet us, bringing gifts of chang, butter and curds. He came along with us, and for the rest of the day he regaled me with memories of the past.

After some miles the path descended into the gorge. We crossed the river by a wooden bridge and climbed steeply through the forest for 2,000 feet to the monastery of Thyangboche, built on the crest of an isolated ridge dominating the junction of the Dudh Kosi and the large tributary valley, the Imja Khola. The ridge was shrouded in mist that evening, and as it was growing dark when we reached the monastery we saw nothing of our surroundings. The monks welcomed us, and we found that a large Tibetan tent had been pitched for us on a meadow nearby.

During the past few days we had become familiar with the extraordinary beauty of the country, but this did not lessen the dramatic effect of the scene which confronted us when we awoke next morning. The sky was clear; the grass of the meadow, starred with gentians, had been touched with frost which sparkled in the early sunlight; the meadow was surrounded by quiet woods of fir, tree-juniper, birch and rhododendron silvered with moss. Though the deciduous trees were still green, there were already brilliant splashes of autumn colour in the undergrowth. To the south the forested slopes fell steeply to the Dudh Kosi, the boom of the river now silenced by the profound depth of the gorge. To the north-east, twelve miles away across the valley of the Imja Khola, stood the Nuptse-Lhotse ridge, with the peak of Everest appearing behind. But even this stupendous wall, nowhere less than 25,000 feet throughout its five-mile length, seemed dwarfed by the slender spires of fluted ice that towered all about us, near and utterly inaccessible.

We stayed in this enchanting spot till noon and visited the monastery during the morning. With its cloistered courtyard, its dark rooms smelling of joss sticks and the rancid butter used for prayer lamps, its terrifying effigies, its tapestries and its holy books bound between boards, it resembled most Tibetan monasteries in all save its setting. In the centre of the main room or shrine there were two thrones, one for the Abbott of Thyangboche, the other for the Abbott of Rongbuk. At that time the former was away on a visit to his colleague on the northern side of the mountain, Chomolungma (Everest). Hanging in one of the windows of the courtyard, we were amused to find an oxygen cylinder. This had evidently been retrieved from the East Rongbuk Glacier by the Sherpas of one of the early Everest expeditions. It is now used as a gong which is sounded each evening at five o'clock as a signal for all the women who happen to be there to leave the monastery.

From Thyangboche the way led gently downwards through the woods and across the Imja Khola at a point where the river plunges as a waterfall into a deep abyss, overhung by gnarled and twisted trees with long beards of moss waving in the spray. Beyond the village of Pangboche we left the forest behind and entered highland country of heath and coarse grass. We spent the night of the 26th at Pheriche, a grazing village then deserted, and on the morning of the 27th we turned into the Lobujya Khola, the valley which contains the Khumbu Glacier. As we climbed into the valley we saw at its head the line of the main watershed. I recognised immediately the peaks and saddles so familiar to us from the Rongbuk side: Pumori, Lingtren, the Lho La, the North Peak and the west shoulder of Everest. It is curious that Angtharkay, who knew these features as well as I did from the other side and had spent many years of his boyhood grazing yaks in this valley, had never recognised them as the same; nor did he do so now until I pointed them out to him. This is a striking example of how little interest Asiatic mountain peasants take in the peaks and ranges around them.

Two days were spent moving slowly up the glacier and getting to know the upper part of the valley. The weather was fine each morning, but each afternoon we had a short, sharp snowstorm. We had some difficulty in finding water along the lateral moraine, but eventually we found a spring in a little sheltered hollow on the west bank of the glacier at the foot of Pumori, and we established our base camp there at an altitude of about 18,000 feet. Later we found that the spring was fed from a small lake a few hundred feet above. There was a small heather-like plant growing on the moraine which served as fuel and supplemented the supplies of juniper that we had brought from below.

On 30 September, Riddiford, Ward and Bourdillon, with two Sherpas, Pasang and Nima, crossed the glacier to reconnoitre the lower part of the icefall. Hillary and I climbed one of the buttresses of Pumori so as to study the icefall as a whole and, in particular, to examine the position of the hanging glaciers on either side of the gorge leading into the Cwm, and to plot the areas of potential danger from ice avalanches falling from these. We reached a height of just over 20,000 feet. It was a wonderful viewpoint. We could see right across the Lho La to the North Peak and the North Col. The whole of the north-west face of Everest was visible, and with our powerful binoculars we could follow every step of the route by which all attempts to climb the mountain had been made. How strange it seemed to be looking at all those well-remembered features from this new angle, and after so long an interval of time and varied experience; the little platform at 25,700 feet where we had spent so many uncomfortable nights, Norton's Camp 6 at the head of the north-east spur, the Yellow Band and the grim overhanging cliffs of the Black Band, the Second Step and the Great Couloir. They were all deep in powder snow as when I had last seen them in 1938. Straight across from where we stood, Nuptse looked superb, a gigantic pyramid of terraced ice.

But the most remarkable and unexpected aspect of the view was that we could see right up to the head of the West Cwm, the whole of the west face of Lhotse, the South Col and the slopes leading up to it. Indeed, a view from the interior of the Cwm itself could hardly have shown us more. We estimated that the floor of the Cwm at its head was nearly 23,000 feet, about 2,000 feet higher than we had expected. From there we could see that there was a perfectly straightforward route up the face of Lhotse to about 25,000 feet, whence, it seemed, a traverse could be made to the South Col. This long traverse would only be feasible in good snow conditions, and at present conditions were obviously anything but good.

The sudden discovery of a practicable route from the West Cwm to the South Col was most exciting. But we had come here to study the icefall, and this occupation soon sobered our spirits. The total height of this frozen cataract was about 2,000 feet. A rough transverse corridor divided it into two equal sections. The glacier descended from the Cwm in a left-hand spiral, so that the lower section of the icefall was facing our viewpoint while the upper half was largely in profile. With the field glasses we picked up two figures on the lower part. From their movements we recognised them, even at that distance, as Riddiford and Pasang. Of the others there was no sign. We heard later that they had taken a different route across the lower glacier and had been forced to turn back by a mass of ice pinnacles before reaching the foot of the icefall. Riddiford and Pasang had made splendid progress, though they were obviously having to work very hard in the soft snow. By two o'clock they had reached a point about four-fifths of the way up the lower section. Here they stayed for an hour and then returned.

Such excellent progress by a party of only two at the very first essay was in itself most encouraging. But from where we were standing, it looked as though the corridor above them was in danger of being swept throughout its length by ice avalanches falling from a great line of hanging glaciers on the left-hand wall of the gorge; it looked, indeed, as though the surface of the corridor was composed entirely of avalanche debris. The right-hand side of the lower icefall and of the corridor were clearly menaced from a mass of hanging glaciers in that direction, while our profile view of the upper icefall made it look very ugly. There was an easy way round the upper icefall to the left, but this was obviously a deathtrap.

One of the many reasons why an attempt upon a great Himalayan peak offers so very much less chance of success than climbing a mountain of Alpine size is that a great part of the route has to be traversed again and again by parties of laden men carrying supplies to the higher camps. All objective dangers must be judged from this standpoint. The risk, say, of walking for ten minutes under an unstable ice tower, which might be accepted by a party of two or three unladen mountaineers, is obviously increased a hundred-fold in the case of large parties of heavily laden men passing over the same ground dozens of times. The rules of mountaineering must be rigidly observed.

It now seemed that we would be faced with a most difficult decision: to abandon this wonderful new route to the summit of Everest that had appeared like a vision, this chance that we had scarcely dared to hope for, not because the way to it was beyond our powers, but because on a small section of the approach the party, and particularly the Sherpas, must repeatedly be exposed to the risk, however slight at each individual exposure, of extermination.

When we met Riddiford in camp that evening he was much more optimistic about the difficulties on the upper part of the icefall, but he had not been in a position to judge the avalanche danger. On the following day (1 October), while Bourdillon and Angtharkay repeated our visit to the Pumori ridge and climbed to a point some 300 feet higher, Hillary and I made a reconnaissance from another angle. This time we went up to the head of the glacier and climbed again to about 20,000 feet on a ridge of the peak bounding the Lho La on the west. From here, although we could not see into the cwm, we had a much better view of the upper part of the icefall and of the corridor. We saw that, at this time of year at any rate, the avalanches from the left swept rather less than half the length of the corridor and that a crossing made at about its centre would be reasonably safe. We could also trace a good route through the upper part of the icefall.

On 2 October, Riddiford, Hillary, Bourdillon and I, with three Sherpas (Pasang, Dannu and Utsering), took a light camp up to the foot of the icefall with the intention of making a concentrated attempt to climb from there into the West Cwm. At this time Murray and Ward were both still suffering from the effects of altitude and remained at the base camp for further acclimatisation. The next day the weather was bad. It snowed gently most of the day and we stayed in our tents. The air about us was absolutely calm. At about ten o'clock we heard a dull roar which sounded like an underground railway train. At first we thought it was a distant avalanche somewhere high up in the cwm. We were quite accustomed to the thunder of these, falling intermittently all around us, from Nuptse, from the great ice-cliffs of the Lho La and from the ridges of Pumori. As a rule, the noise did not last more than a minute or two at a time. When, after a quarter of an hour, this distant roar was still maintained, we began to think that somewhere far away an entire mountainside must be collapsing. However, after an hour, even this theory seemed hardly tenable, and eventually we came to the conclusion that it must be caused by a mighty wind blowing across the Lho La and over the ridges of Everest and Nuptse. It went on throughout the day. No breeze ruffled the canvas of our tents.

The morning of the 4th was fine and very cold. We started soon after it was light. As we had anticipated, one of the difficulties of working on the icefall, particularly at this time of year, was the fact that the sun reached it so late in the day. At first, we were moving over hard ice, but as soon as we reached the icefall we were up to our knees in soft snow. Our feet became very cold, and once during the morning Hillary and Riddiford had to remove their boots, which were designed for their summer expedition and were only large enough for two pairs of socks, to have their feet massaged back to life. With Riddiford's tracks to follow, we had no difficulty in finding our way through the maze of crevasses and ice-walls. After three-and-a-half hours' steady going, we reached his farthest point. Here Bourdillon, who was also still suffering a good deal from the effects of altitude, decided to stop and await our return. The place was just beside a prominent ice-tower which was thereafter known as 'Tom's Sérac'. As the sun was now up, he would be able to keep warm enough.

Indeed, our trouble was now exactly the reverse. With the scorching glare of the sun on the fresh snow and the stagnant air among the ice-cliffs, it was rather like working in front of a furnace. This, combined with the altitude, very soon drained our energy and robbed all movement of pleasure. We shed all our upper garments except our shirts, but even so we poured with sweat, and before long our panting produced a tormenting thirst. The going now became far more complicated and laborious. Threading our way through a wild laby-rinth of ice walls, chasms and towers, we could rarely see more than 200 feet ahead. The snow was often hip-deep, so that even with so many to share the labour of making the trail, progress from point to point was very slow. The choice of one false line alone cost us an hour of fruitless toil.

But technically the climbing was not difficult, and even if it had been we had plenty of time for the job. By the middle of the afternoon we seemed to be approaching the top of the icefall. We had decided to turn back not later than four o'clock in order to reach camp by six, when it would be getting too dark to see. Even that was running it rather fine, since it did not allow for accidents, such as the breaking of a snow bridge, and to become involved in such a com-plication after dark would be to run considerable risk of frostbite.

From the last line of séracs we looked across a deep trough to a level crest of ice marking the point where the glacier of the cwm took its first plunge into the icefall, like the smooth wave above a waterfall. The trough was really a wide crevasse, partly choked by huge ice blocks, some of which appeared none too stable. Crossing it was the most delicate operation we had encountered.

By 3.50 we reached the final slope beyond the trough, less than 100 feet below the crest, from which we expected to have a clear view along the gently sloping glacier of the cwm. We had to climb this diagonally to the right, so as to avoid a vertical brow of ice directly above. Pasang, whose turn it was, took over the lead; Riddiford followed and I came next. When we were on the slope it became obvious that the snow was most unstable and must be treated with great caution. By this time Pasang had advanced about sixty feet. Suddenly the surface began to slide downwards, breaking into blocks as it went. Pasang, who was at the upper edge of the break, managed with great skill to dive over it and ram his ice axe into the snow above. I was only a few yards from Hillary, who had a firm anchorage on an ice block at the beginning of the slope, and I was able without much difficulty to scramble off the moving slope back to him. Riddiford went down with the slope, and was left suspended between Pasang and me, while the avalanche slid silently into the trough. It was a nasty little incident, which might with less luck have had rather unpleasant consequences.

It was now high time to retreat. Going down was, of course, almost effortless compared with the labour of coming up. We had the deep trail to follow and we could jump or glissade down the innumerable little cliffs, each of which had cost a great deal of time and hard work to climb. It was after 5.30 when we reached Bourdillon, who had had a longer wait than he had bargained for, and was by now getting both cold and anxious. Soon after we had started down, the icefall became enveloped in mist. Later, this broke behind us and we saw, high above the darkening cwm, the north face of Nuptse, a golden tracery of ice lit by the setting sun. We reached camp as it was getting dark, very tired after a strenuous day.

We were well satisfied with this reconnaissance. It was rather disappointing at the last moment to be denied a view into the cwm from the top of the icefall, though in fact it would not have shown us much more than we had seen already. But we had climbed practically the whole of the icefall in a single day, despite abominable snow conditions and the fact that for the largest and most difficult part we had been working our way over entirely new ground. In time the route could certainly be greatly improved, and the climb would then be done in half the time and with less than half the effort. We thought that the snow conditions would probably improve, but even if they did not, the final slope could certainly be climbed and safeguarded by suspending lifelines from above. Finally, at this time of year at least, the route seemed to be reasonably free from the menace of ice avalanches. We had little doubt that, with a few days' work, we could construct a safe packing route up the icefall into the West Cwm.

We decided, however, to wait for a fortnight before attempting to do this. There were three reasons for this decision. The first was to allow time for snow conditions on the icefall to improve. Secondly, we had seen that there was still an enormous amount of monsoon snow lying on the upper slopes of Lhotse and Everest which would make it impossible to climb far towards the South Col, to say nothing of the possible risk of large snow avalanches falling into the cwm from above. While we knew that at altitudes of 23,000 feet and above this snow would not consolidate, we had reason to believe that by the beginning of November a great deal of it would have been removed by the northwesterly winds which were already becoming established. Finally, half the party were badly in need of acclimatisation before they could undertake any serious work even in the icefall. We spent the fortnight making journeys into the unexplored country to the west and south.

On 19 October, Hillary and I, who had been working together during this fortnight, returned to the Base Camp on the Khumbu Glacier. We had expected the others to get back on the same date, but they did not arrive until nearly a week later. On the 20th and 21st we took a camp to the old site at the foot of the icefall. This time we brought with us a large twelve-man double-skinned dome tent designed for the Arctic. It was well worth the labour required to level a sufficiently large area of the ice surface on which to pitch it, for, after the tiny mountain tents we had been using hitherto, it was positively luxurious, and, having more room, we found it a great deal easier to get off to a really early start in the morning. On the 22nd we started work on the icefall. Snow conditions had improved slightly, but a number of new crevasses had opened up across our former route, and these caused us a little trouble to negotiate. However, by the end of the first day's work we had made a solid and completely safe route up as far as 'Tom's Sérac'. Near this we marked out a site for a light camp from which to work on the upper part of the icefall, but we decided that for the present we would continue to work from our comfortable camp below.

On the 23rd we started early, taking with us Angtharkay and Utsering. It was a glorious morning. With every step of the way prepared, we climbed without effort, breathing no faster than on a country walk at home, and reached 'Tom's Sérac' in one hour and twenty minutes. We paused there for a brief rest that we hardly needed, while the sun climbed above the great Nuptse-Lhotse ridge to quicken the frozen world about us. We were in a mood of exultant confidence, for we expected that very day to enter the great cwm.

But immediately above the sérac we ran into difficulties. A broad crevasse had opened across our former route, and it took us an hour and a half and a lot of very hard work to find a way across it. This check, though a salutary warning against overconfidence, was not serious, and it was not until we were over the crevasse that the real trouble began. Here, about 100 yards from the sérac, we found that a tremendous change had taken place. Over a wide area the cliffs and towers that had been there before had been shattered as though by an earthquake, and now lay in a tumbled ruin. This had evidently been caused by a sudden movement of the main mass of the glacier which had occurred some time during the last fortnight. It was impossible to avoid the sober reflection that if we had persisted with the establishment of a line of communication through the icefall and if a party had happened to be in the area at the time, it was doubtful whether any of them would have survived. Moreover, the same thing might happen on other parts of the icefall.

With regard to our immediate problem, however, we hoped that the collapse of the ice had left the new surface with a solid foundation, though it was so broken and alarming in appearance. Very gingerly, prodding with our ice axes at every step, with 100 feet of rope between each man, we ventured across the shattered area. The whole thing felt very unsound, but it was difficult to tell whether the instability was localised around the place one was treading or whether it applied to the area as a whole. Hillary was ahead, chopping his way through the ice blocks, when one of these, a small one, fell into a void below. There was a prolonged roar and the surface on which we stood began to shudder violently. I thought it was about to collapse, and the Sherpas, somewhat irrationally perhaps, flung themselves to the ground. In spite of this alarming experience, it was not so much the shattered area that worried us as the part beyond, where the cliffs and séracs were riven by innumerable new cracks which seemed to threaten a further collapse. We retreated to the sound ice below and attempted to find a less dangerous route. Any extensive movement to the left would have brought us under fire from the hanging glaciers in that direction. We explored the ground to the right, but here we found that the area of devastation was far more extensive. It was overhung, moreover, by a line of extremely unstable séracs.

We returned to camp in a very different frame of mind from the joyous mood in which we had climbed the lower part of the icefall only a few hours before. It seemed obvious that, though it might be a permissible risk for a party of unladen mountaineers, working on long ropes and taking every available precaution, to attempt the icefall, and even this was doubtful, we would not be justified in trying to climb it with a party of laden porters whose movements are always difficult to control. It looked as though, after all, we were to be faced with the decision which we had dreaded three or four weeks before: to abandon the attempt to reach the cwm, not because the way was difficult, but because of a danger, which by the very nature of its underlying causes was impossible to assess with any certainty. In this case, however, it did not mean the total abandonment of the route; for the condition of icefalls is subject to considerable seasonal variation, and it was not unreasonable to expect much better conditions in the spring than in the autumn. Nevertheless, it was a bitter disappointment not to be able to proceed with our plan of carrying a camp through into the cwm and making a close examination of the route to the South Col. We agreed, however, to defer the final decision until we had made another reconnaissance of the icefall with the whole party.

The following day we again climbed the ridge near the Lho La. The view was not very encouraging, for we could see no way of avoiding the shattered area, which was in fact a belt stretching right across the glacier; though the upper part of the icefall above the corridor, so far as we could see, was undisturbed. On the 26th the rest of the party arrived back at the Base Camp, and on the 27th we all climbed the ridge of Pumori from which Hillary and I had first looked into the West Cwm on 30 September. We saw that a certain amount of monsoon snow had been removed by the north-west wind from the peak of Everest, though the north face of the mountain was still in an unclimbable condition. There was no apparent change in the snow conditions inside the cwm, on Lhotse or on the South Col.

That evening we reoccupied the camp below the icefall, and on 28 October all six of us, together with Angtharkay, Pasang and Nima, set out for the icefall once more. Our chief object was that the others should examine the situation for themselves so that we could come to a united decision; though Hillary and I, too, were anxious to have another look at it. We arrived at the shattered area by the time the sun reached us. Only minor changes had taken place in the past five days, and this encouraged us, with great care, to cross it and make our way over the delicately poised séracs beyond. Pasang and Angtharkay made no secret of their apprehension and constantly pointed out to me that it was no place to take laden men. Beyond the corridor we found that the upper icefall was in a fairly stable condition, only one sérac having collapsed across our former route. By ten o'clock we reached the final wall dominating the icefall. The steep slopes below this were in the same dangerous condition as they had been at the beginning of the month; but a fin of ice had become detached from the wall, and while other routes were being explored, Bourdillon succeeded in cutting steps up this, thus enabling us to reach the top of the wall. This was a fine effort, for it involved cutting his way through a deep layer of unstable snow into the ice beneath. By keeping to the edge of the fin, he was able to avoid any risk of a snow avalanche, but, as the whole thing overhung a profound chasm into which it might collapse, it was as well to avoid having more than one man on it at a time.

We now stood above the icefall, on the lip of the West Cwm, and we could look up the gently sloping glacier between the vast walls of Everest and Nuptse to its head. But we soon found that we had by no means overcome all the difficulties of entry into this curious sanctuary. A little way farther on a vast crevasse split the glacier from side to side, and there were indications of others equally formidable beyond. To cross these in their present state would have taken many days of hard work and a good deal of ingenuity, and unless we could carry a camp up to this point we were not in a position to tackle them. I have little doubt that in the spring they would be a great deal easier. We sat for nearly an hour contemplating the white, silent amphitheatre and the magnificent view across the Khumbu Glacier to Pumori, Lingtren and the peaks beyond the Lho La. Then we returned down the icefall.

The fact that we had now climbed the icefall without mishap made the decision to abandon the attempt to carry supplies through into the Cwm all the more difficult. We discussed it at great length. The next day Ward and Bourdillon climbed the ridge near the Lho La to satisfy themselves that there was no alternative route, while Hillary and I paid one more visit to the icefall. Angtharkay and Pasang were still convinced that it would be madness in the present conditions to try to carry loads through it, and unfair to ask the Sherpas to do so. There was nothing for it but to submit, hoping that we would get another chance in the spring.

4   Exploratory Journeys

Our failure to make a safe route up the icefall, and so to bring camps and supplies through into the West Cwm, disappointing though it was, had one great consolation, for it allowed us more time than we might otherwise have had to explore some of the great areas of unknown country along the southern side of the main range. During the period between our two visits to the icefall we divided into two parties. Murray, Riddiford, Bourdillon and Ward made their way westward from the Base Camp, up a long tributary glacier which took them past Pumori and along the southern side of the watershed. Apart from the exploration of the area, their chief object was to find a pass across the range to the north, which the Sherpas had told us about. We assumed that it must lead over to the West Rongbuk glacier, and it was hoped that the party might be able to climb Pumori from there. I was particularly interested in this alleged pass in view of our failure in 1935 to find any route across this part of the range. They found, however, that no such pass existed.

From the head of the tributary glacier they crossed a col which led them into the upper basin of the Dudh Kosi, at the head of which they found themselves in a mighty cirque formed by the two great mountains of Cho Oyu (26,750 feet) and Gyachung Kang (25,910 feet). On the eastern flank of this cirque was the Nup La, which had been reached by Hazard from the Tibetan side in 1924. For two days they climbed towards this col up an icefall, a good deal more difficult than the West Cwm icefall, though much less dangerous, before they finally gave up their attempt to reach the watershed. Then they descended the Ngojumbo Glacier and the valley of the Dudh Kosi to Namche.

Meanwhile, Hillary and I explored the country to the south of Mount Everest. Our chief objective was to find a way through the tangle of ranges to the Kangshung glacier which flows from the eastern flanks of Everest, and so to link up with the explorations of the 1921 Reconnaissance Expedition. In this project we were stimulated by the Sherpas' statement that at the head of the Imja Khola there was a pass leading over to Kharta in Tibet. We took with us a young man called Ang Doije, who knew that valley well and who was most insistent that the pass existed. The upper basin of the Imja is contained on the north by the Nuptse-Lhotse wall and on the east and south by dozens of unnamed peaks between 20,000 feet and 24,000 feet high. When we reached its head we saw at once that there was no practicable way across the mountains to the east. Ang Dorje was not in the least abashed, and merely said that he had supposed that we, as mountaineers, would find a way. Turning southwards, however, we succeeded with some difficulty in crossing a col about 19,000 feet high over into the basin of the Hongu Khola, where we camped on the shores of a big lake. We looked across a wide basin to the Chamlang peaks. We were now well beyond the country known to the Sherpas, but we found evidence that the Hindu Nepalis from the south penetrated with their flocks to these valleys.

We crossed the Hongu basin to the eastward and found a pass, about 20,300 feet high, leading over to the great Barun Glacier flowing south-eastwards at the foot of Makalu (27,790 feet). From here, if we had had another three days' food with us, we could undoubtedly have reached the Kangshung. Another tempting project that presented itself, if only we had had the time and resources to undertake it, was to descend the Barun and to plunge into the great unexplored gorges leading down to the Arun River. But, once embarked upon this game of mountain exploration in these remote ranges, there is no end to its fascinating possibilities.

All this time the weather was fine and the period spanned the full moon. The nights were very cold. The mornings were sparkling clear; each afternoon cloud welled up out of the valleys and wrapped the peaks; each evening at sunset it dissolved. It was then, in camp, that we saw this stupendous country at its best, for each peak in turn was framed in shifting mists, its golden tracery of ice glowing in deep relief; no longer a mere part of a mountain massif, but floating in sublime isolation. Before the cloud had quite vanished, the moon would climb above some lofty crest, and presently all the peaks were there again, frozen against the night sky.

Returning across the Hongu basin, we crossed a third pass, also about 20,000 feet, on its western rim just to the south of the beautiful peak of Ama Dablam, which, as we had hoped, took us back into the valley of the Imja Khola. Finally, we crossed a high ridge running southward from Nuptse and so back to our Base Camp on the Khumbu Glacier.

Our third field of activity was the Gauri Sankar range, which we set out to explore at the beginning of November after work on the icefall had been abandoned. We went north-west from Namche along the valley of the Bhote Kosi. At Thame, Hillary, Riddiford and Dutt, who during October had been carrying out extensive geological investigations over a wide area, turned up a valley to the west and crossed the Tesi Lapcha. This pass, though involving some difficult ice climbing, was known to and occasionally used by the Sherpas. It led through a mass of spectacular granite peaks over a northerly offshoot of the main range into a most remarkable gorge, known as the Rolwaling, running westward under the southern precipices of Gauri Sankar. The rest of us continued along the Bhote Kosi to the little grazing village of Chhule. From here

Murray and Bourdillon, taking four days' food with them, went on to visit the Nangpa La, the pass by which the trade route crosses from Sola Khumbu to Tibet. It is approached on either side of the watershed up a long glacier and is situated in an extensive icefield at an altitude of more than 19,000 feet. It is, so far as I know, the highest pass on any trade route in the world. It carries a considerable volume of traffic throughout most of the year, and deep grooves worn in the glacier ice bear witness to the passage of countless yaks. No ponies are taken across, not because it is too high, for ponies are used extensively in the Karakoram Pass, which is not much lower, but because of a curious superstition that if anyone attempts to take a pony across, not only will the pony die, but the owner also will perish. It is by way of the Nangpa La that the Sherpas have their intimate contact with Tibet; large numbers of them cross it every year, not only to trade, but to make a pilgrimage to the Rongbuk Monastery. From near the pass, Murray and Bourdillon saw a possible way of climbing Cho Oyu.

From Chhule, Ward and I made our way westward into a group of high mountains whose position in relation to the main range was difficult to determine. After some time spent in reconnaissance, we found what seemed to be the only way through them, over a col which we subsequently named the Menlung La. Travelling very light and taking enough food for a week, we crossed this col together with Sen Tensing. It led over to a large glacier system, the main ice-stream of which was flowing southward, which suggested that we were still on the southern side of the main range. However, when we came to explore our new surroundings, we found that we were in a vast amphitheatre, in many respects very like the Nanda Devi basin, in the centre of which, completely isolated from the main massif, stood a most lovely peak of pale granite. It was the highest peak of the range, being somewhat higher than Gauri Sankar. We named it 'Menlungtse'. We found that the waters of the basin drained to the north-west and plunged directly into a system of tremendous canyons, the main artery of which we identified as the Rongshar. It is one of those remarkable rivers which, like the Arun, rise far to the north on the Tibetan plateau and have cut their way clean through the great Himalayan range. It is certainly one of the most spectacular gorges I have seen. We also succeeded in reaching the crest of the main range south of 'Menlungtse' at a point about 19,500 feet high. From here we looked straight down 7,000 feet into the Rolwaling. Sen Tensing told me that this name was a Sherpa word meaning the furrow made by a plough. We were surprised to find that there was a way down the huge precipices into the gorge.

It was on one of the glaciers of the Menlung basin, at a height of about 19,000 feet, that, late one afternoon, we came across those curious footprints in the snow, the report of which has caused a certain amount of public interest in Britain. We did not follow them further than was convenient, a mile or so, for we were carrying heavy loads at the time, and besides we had reached a particularly interesting stage in the exploration of the basin. I have in the past found many sets of these curious footprints and have tried to follow them, but have always lost them on the moraine or rocks at the side of the glacier. These particular ones seemed to be very fresh, probably not more than twenty-four hours old. When Murray and Bourdillon followed us a few days later the tracks had been almost obliterated by melting. Sen Tensing, who had no doubt whatever that the creatures (for there had been at least two) that had made the tracks were 'Yetis' or wild men, told me that two years before, he and a number of other Sherpas had seen one of them at a distance of about twenty-five yards at Thyangboche. He described it as half man and half beast, standing about five feet six inches, with a tall pointed head, its body covered with reddish brown hair, but with a hairless face. When we reached Kathmandu at the end of November, I had him cross-examined in Nepali (I conversed with him in Hindustani). He left no doubt as to his sincerity. Whatever it was that he had seen, he was convinced that it was neither a bear nor a monkey, with both of which animals he was, of course, very familiar. Of the various theories that have been advanced to account for these tracks, the only one which is in any way plausible is that they were made by a langur monkey, and even this is very far from convincing, as I believe those who have suggested it would be the first to admit.

These various exploratory journeys gave us an intimate knowledge of a stretch of sixty miles of the Great Himalaya Range, in a country hitherto practically unknown to Western travellers. This form of mountaineering, the exploration of unknown peaks, glaciers and valleys, the finding and crossing of new passes to connect one area with another, is the most fascinating occupation I know. The variety of experience, the constantly changing scene, the gradual unfolding of the geography of the range are deeply satisfying, for they yield a very real understanding, almost a sense of personal possession, of the country explored.

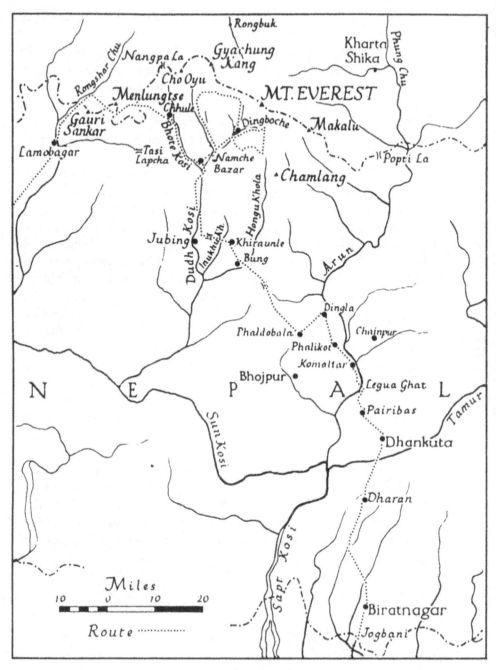

The route of the approach march.

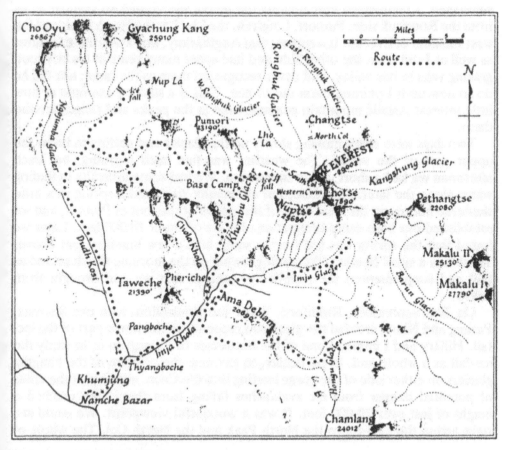

Explorations in the Everest district.

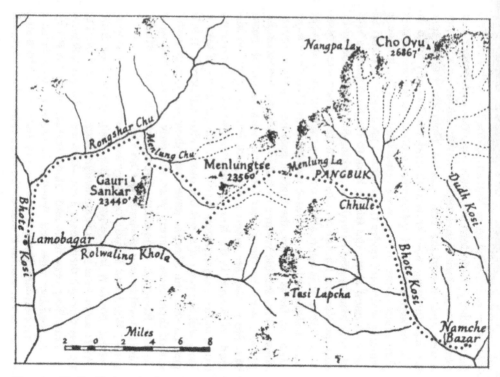

The routes of the Gauri Sankar exploration.

The Khumbu Icefall – 'riven with cracks that seemed to threaten collapse'.

The 1951 Everest Reconnaissance Expedition approached the mountain from the south: a bathe before crossing the Arun River in a huge dugout canoe.

The first comprehensive view of the Western Cwm, from the slopes of Pumori.

Members of the 1951 Everest Reconnaissance Expedition: Eric Shipton (left), W.H. Murray, Tom Bourdillon, Earle Riddiford (and seated) Michael Ward and Edmund Hillary.

Menlungste (23,560 feet), the unclimbed peak west of Everest. 'We were in a vast amphitheatre in the centre of which stood the most lovely peak of pale granite'.

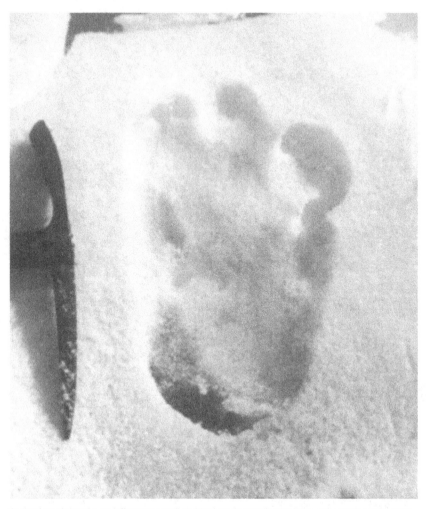

On the glacier below this peak Shipton's party found fresh tracks providing evidence of the existence of the Yeti.

Printed in the USA
CPSIA information can be obtained
at www.ICGtesting.com
JSHW012017140824
68134JS00025B/2467